CLUELESS IN TOKYO

AN EXPLORER'S SKETCHBOOK OF
WEIRD AND WONDERFUL THINGS
IN JAPAN

BY BETTY REYNOLDS

NEW YORK · Weatherhill · TOKYO

To my husband Frank, whose career brought us
to this strange and wonderful place, and to our many new
friends in Japan who tried their very best to enlighten us
and to my editor, Ray Furse...

Domo arigato gozaimasu!

Thank you!

- First edition, 1997
Fifth printing, 2001
Published by Weatherhill, Inc, of New York and Tokyo

Library of Congress Cataloging-in-Publication Data
Reynolds, Betty.
Clueless in Tokyo: an explorer's sketch book of weird and wonderful
things in Tokyo/ by Betty Reynolds--1st ed.
p. cm.
ISBN 0-8348-0386-0
1. Japan--Social life and customs--1945-- pictorial works.
I. Title.
DS822 5.R48 1977
952--dc21
96-48871
CIP

Irasshaimase!
Welcome!

Welcome to Japan, a place where assuming you're not Japanese, everything is completely different from back home. It certainly was for me when I arrived two years ago.

Clueless in Tokyo is a sketchbook and journal of my delightfully disorienting encounter with Japan, and I hope it will be useful, or at least entertaining for others fortunate enough to have the same experience. It is a book for those planning to visit Japan and curious about what they will see, as well as for those with no plans to go, but who want to know what all the fuss is about.

Goran Kudasai!
Please take a look!

Tanuki

A symbol of good times, this ceramic badger was modeled after the sons of rich Edo merchants known for their debauches with sake and loose women

Kokeshi

These dolls originally represented spirits of the gods but their endearing faces made them popular folk toys

WHAT ARE THOSE DOLLS WITH THE PAINTED FACES AND NO ARMS?

WHO'S THAT WEIRD CREATURE LURKING IN THE DOORWAYS OF BARS AND RESTAURANTS? AND WHY DO

WHO'S THAT CAT AND WHY IS SHE WAVING TO ME?

Maneki-neko

This cat isn't waving. She's beckoning in good fortune, saying "Money come, money come"

Henna Yatsu

Curious Characters

Daruma

An Indian monk known for his religious devotion. He lost the use of his legs because he sat in meditation so long

Shichifukujin

The Seven Gods of Good Luck are celebrated during the New Year

WHAT'S THIS RED TOMATO WITH THE BIG EYES?

Paint in one eye and make a wish. When the wish is granted paint in the other eye

Bishamonten

Ebisu Jurōjin Hotei Benzaiten Fukurokuju Daikoku

WHO IS THAT GANG OF SEVEN?

Tera
Mysterious Temples

Senbazuru
Strings of 1000 origami cranes hung to make wishes come true

WHAT ARE THOSE COLORFUL STRANDS HANGING IN THE TEMPLES?

WHAT'S WRITTEN ON THE BACK OF THOSE WOODEN PLAQUES?

WHAT ARE THOSE STICKS PEOPLE SHAKE OUT OF A BOX?

Ema
People buy these votive plaques and write on them their wishes for good things in life

Omizuko
Represent aborted, miscarried or stillborn infants. Colorful caps and pinwheels are donated to console their spirits

mikuji

m of divination
hich the number on
tick corresponds to
rtune written on a
ce of paper

Unlike fortune cookies
the paper fortunes
of omikuji can be
good or bad. They are
often left behind on trees

WHO'S THAT LITTLE GUY I SEE BY THE ROADSIDE EVERYWHERE?

Jizó-sama

The patron saint
and guardian
of dead children

WHAT ARE THOSE STONE STATUES WITH THE HAND-MADE RED CAPS AND BIBS?

WHAT ARE THOSE LIGHTNING BOLTS ON ROPES?

Shimenawa
Ropes of rice straw are symbols marking the boundary between sacred and profane spaces

Gohei
Folded paper o[f] Cloth strips h[ang] as symbolic offerings to the gods

Inari Kitsune
Foxes, usually in pairs, are guardians of the rice goddess

WHO ARE THOSE FOXES SITTING IN FRONT OF THE SHRINE?

Food for the fox

WHAT ARE THOSE STONE P[...]

WHAT IS THAT MELTED SNOWMAN ON THE ALTAR?

Kagami-mochi
Pounded rice cakes representing the sacred mirror, a symbol of the Imperial family

Ishi-dōrō
Stone lanterns placed in front of graves and shrines

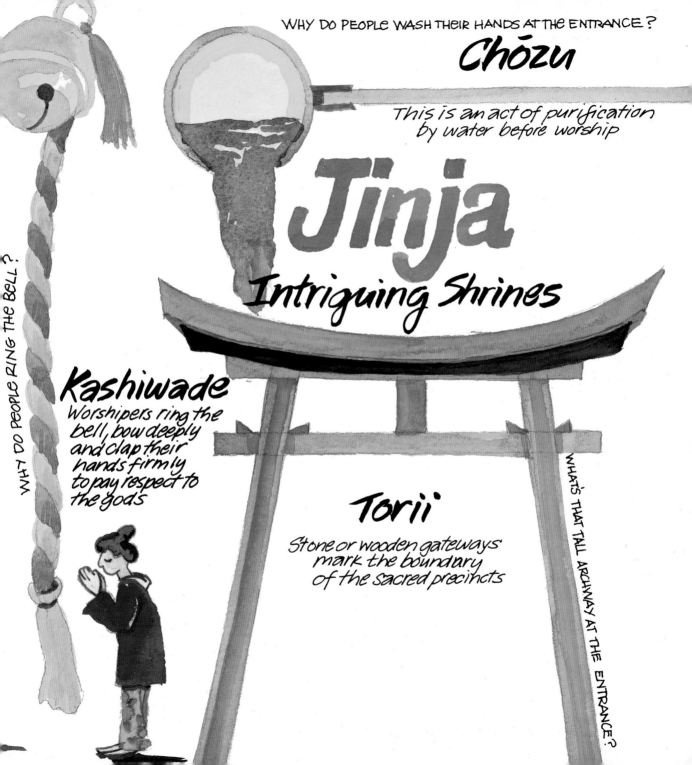

WHY DO PEOPLE WASH THEIR HANDS AT THE ENTRANCE?

Chōzu

This is an act of purification by water before worship

Jinja
Intriguing Shrines

WHY DO PEOPLE RING THE BELL?

Kashiwade

Worshipers ring the bell, bow deeply and clap their hands firmly to pay respect to the gods

Torii

Stone or wooden gateways mark the boundary of the sacred precincts

WHAT'S THAT TALL ARCHWAY AT THE ENTRANCE?

Succulent Sushi

Shōyu
soy sauce

Yikes! Wasabi
Add a modest amount of horseradish to soy sauce for a traditional sushi dip

Sushi is a mound of vinegared rice with raw fish on top

Sashimi is sliced raw fish

Oshibori
Moist hand towel

Hashi
Chopsticks

Gari
Pickled ginger

Maguro
Tuna

Tako
Octopus

Hashioki
Chopstick rest

WHAT'S THE GREEN STUFF THAT BRINGS TEARS TO YOUR EYES?

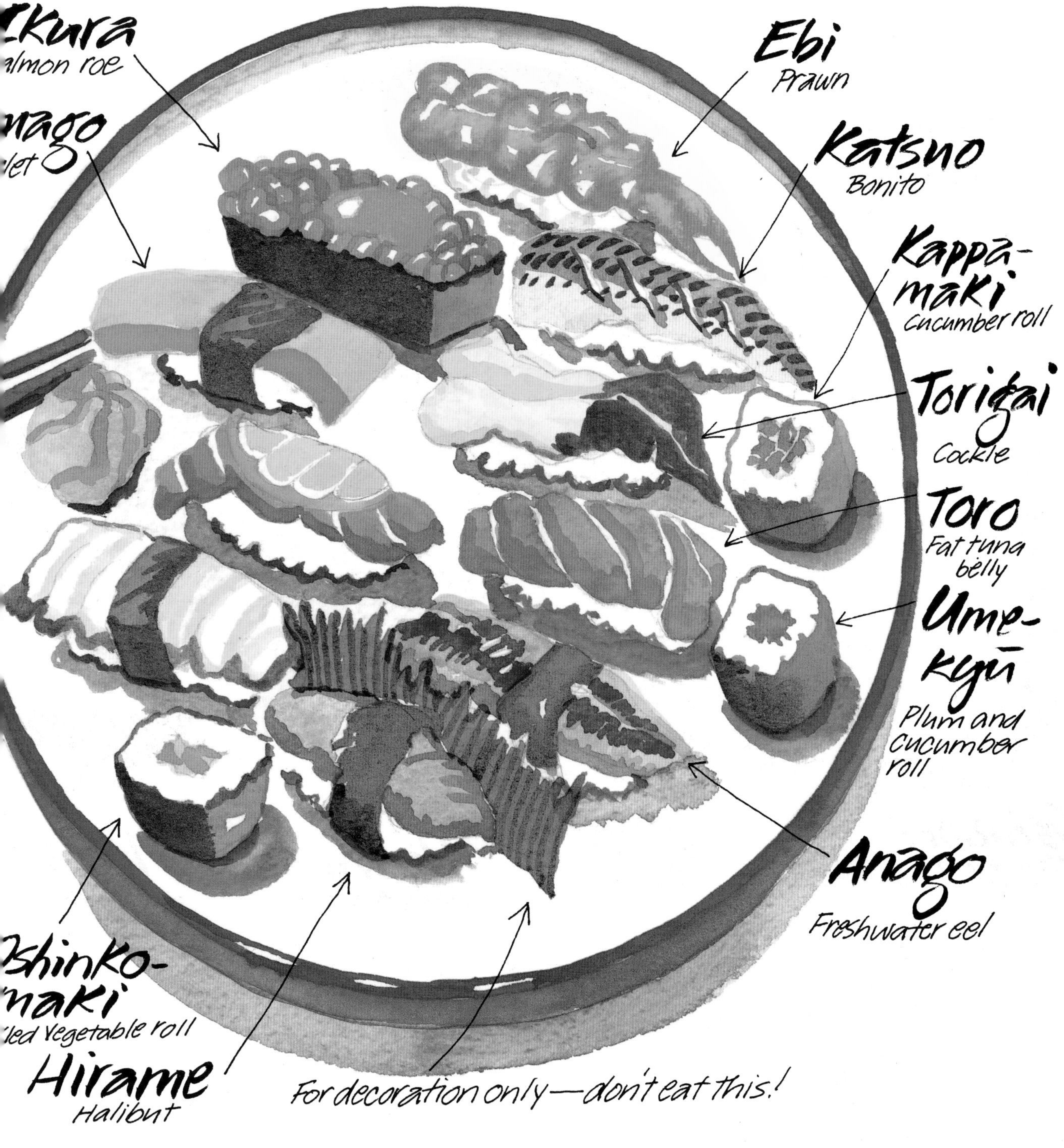

Ikura
Salmon roe

Anago
let

Ebi
Prawn

Katsuo
Bonito

Kappa-maki
Cucumber roll

Torigai
Cockle

Toro
Fat tuna belly

Ume-kyū
Plum and cucumber roll

Anago
Freshwater eel

Oshinko-maki
led Vegetable roll

Hirame
Halibut

For decoration only—don't eat this!

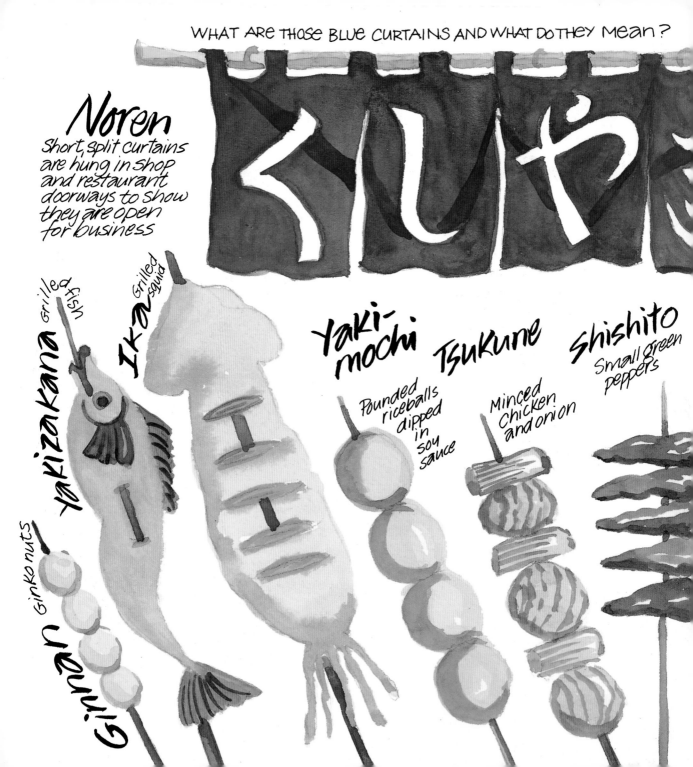

Noren
Short, split curtains are hung in shop and restaurant doorways to show they are open for business

くしゃ

Yakizakana Grilled fish

Ika Grilled squid

Yaki-mochi Pounded riceballs dipped in soy sauce

Tsukune Minced chicken and onion

Shishito Small green peppers

Ginnan Ginko nuts

Kushimono
Dinner on a Stick

Aka-chōchin
Advertise inexpensive eating and drinking places

...aki-...iku
...illed beef

Unagi
Eel

WHAT ARE THE RED LANTERNS HANGING OUTSIDE OF SOME RESTAURANTS?

Ozōni

Pounded rice cakes consumed in a New Year's soup can get lodged in the throat. Ozōni claims several victims each year

Urı
Sea urchin roe

WHY WOULD YOU PAY SO MUCH MO

Shio Kara

Squid innards in a special sauce. Sake is the drink of choice with this delicacy

WHAT BEVERAGE GOES BEST WITH SALTY, SLIMY SQUID GUTS?

Traditional Senryu verse – Last night he and I ate

Tako Fuokachio
Octopus in a pocket

Tako-yaki
Octopus pies

Tako
Octopus is served raw in sushi or cooked in a variety of ways

R.
por
wi
fuguch

Basashi

Raw horsemeat

Kujira-niku

It's not illegal to eat whale in Japan

Fearsome Fugu

Pufferfish and other foods I never thought would pass my lips

...SOMETHING THAT MAY KILL YOU?

...I help carry his coffin

A FUGU MEAL CAN COST $200 OR MORE IN TOKYO

Fugusashi
Thinly sliced raw fugu

Fuguchiri
Fugu soup with veggies

Fugu

The blowfish is considered a delicacy in Japan even though the toxins concentrated in the organs are 275 times deadlier than cyanide. There is no known antidote

Hirezake
Toasted fugu fins in sake causes a slight numbness in the lips and tongue

Buddhist priests offer prayers to fugu to console their spirits

Puchi *Petite tomato*

IS THAT A WEAPON OR A VEGETABLE

Shishr

↳ *Sweet pepper*

Kyūri *Cucumber*

Shōga *Ginger root*

Takenoko

Bamboo shoot

Wasabi *Horseradish*

shimeji *Mushroom*

Yasai

Exotic Veggies

HEY, WHERE ARE THE PEAS?

Gobō *Burdock root*

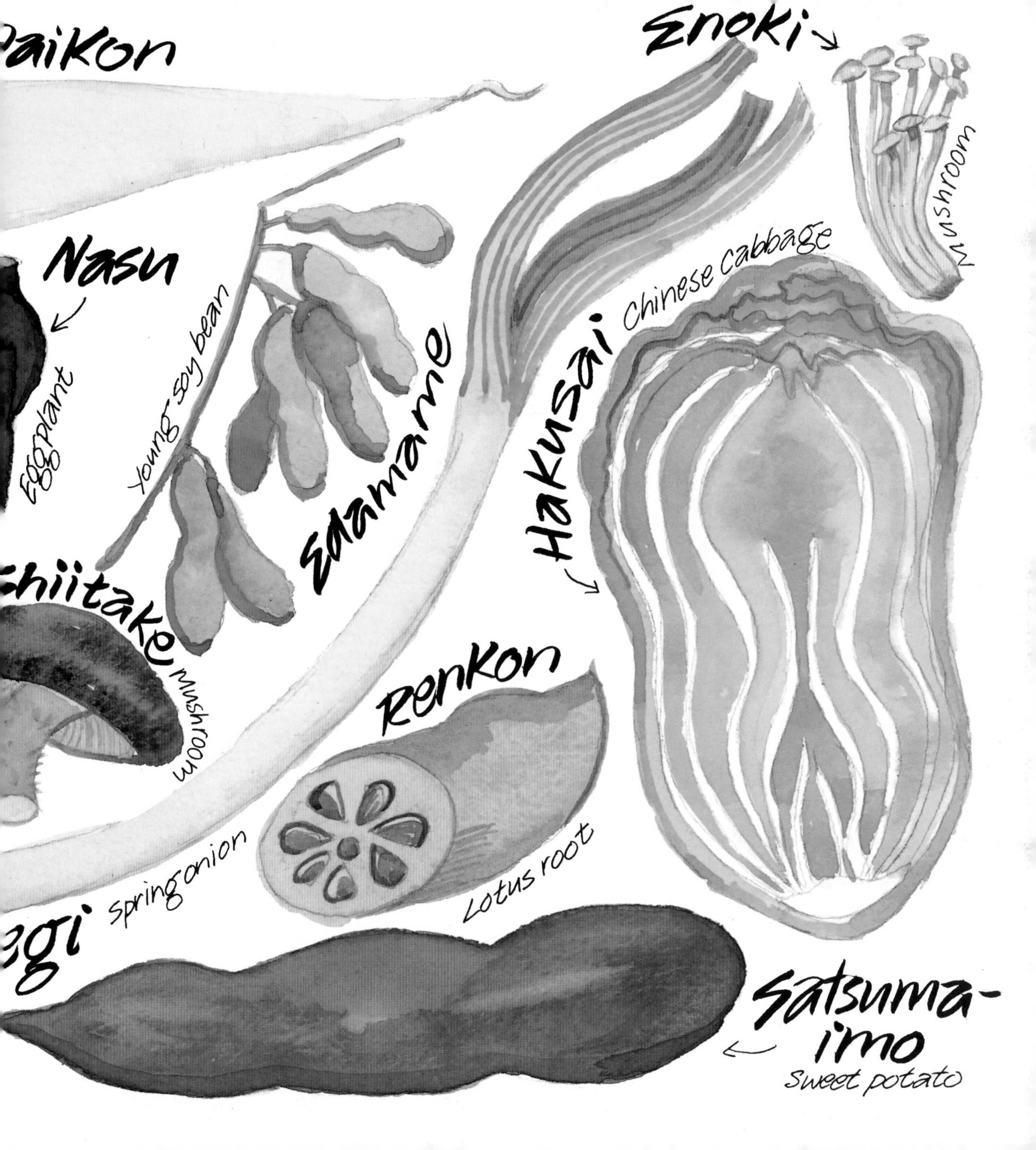

Daikon

Nasu
Eggplant

Young soy bean

Edamame

Shiitake
mushroom

Renkon
Lotus root

egi spring onion

Enoki
mushroom

Hakusai
Chinese cabbage

Satsuma-imo
Sweet potato

Captivating
Kimono

Obi-jime
Cord used
to secure
obi

Haori
Men's formal
jacket

Yukata
Cotton summer
kimono for men
and women

Hakama
Pleated
skirt

Uchiwa
Fan on a stick

. ALWAYS WRAP KIMONO LEFT TO RIGHT SO AS NOT TO BE TAKEN FOR A DEAD PERSON

Sensu
Folding fan

Obi
Kimono
Sash

Furisode
Long-sleeved
kimono worn by
unmarried
women

Tomesode
Formal kimono
for women
after marriage

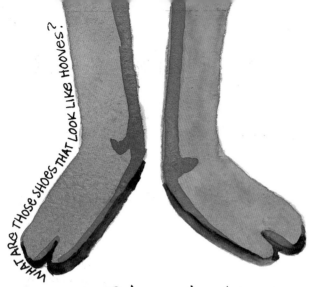 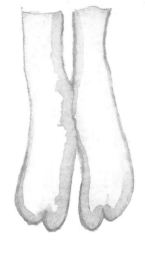 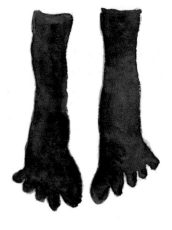

WHAT ARE THOSE SHOES THAT LOOK LIKE HOOVES?

Jika-tabi
Split-toed shoes worn by monks and construction workers

Tabi
Split-toed socks for thonged sandals

Tabi-Kutsushita
Incredible five-toed socks

Sandaru
Outdoor slippers

Surippa
Indoor slippers

Toire-no-Surippa
Toilet slippers

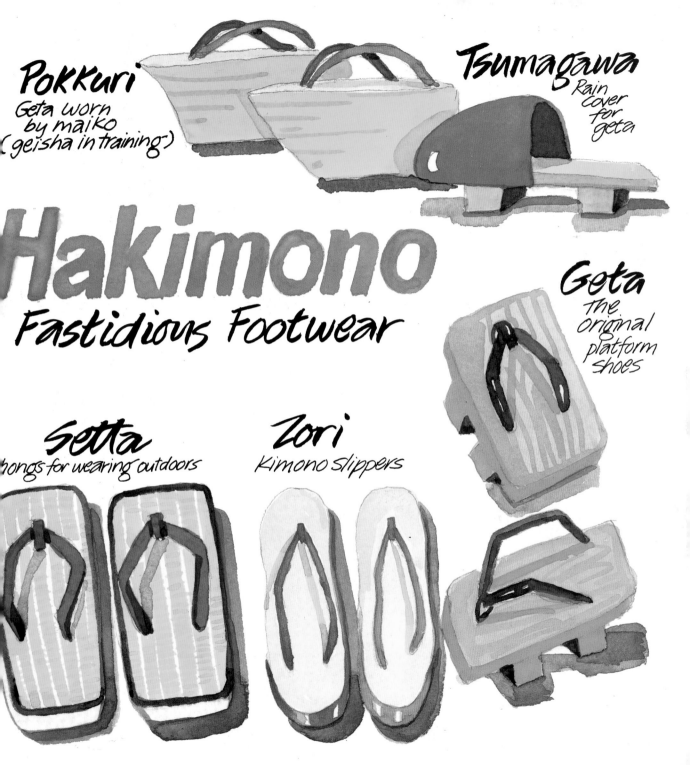

Pokkuri
Geta worn
by maiko
(geisha in training)

Tsumagawa
Rain
cover
for
geta

Hakimono
Fastidious Footwear

Geta
The
original
platform
shoes

Setta
Thongs for wearing outdoors

Zori
Kimono slippers

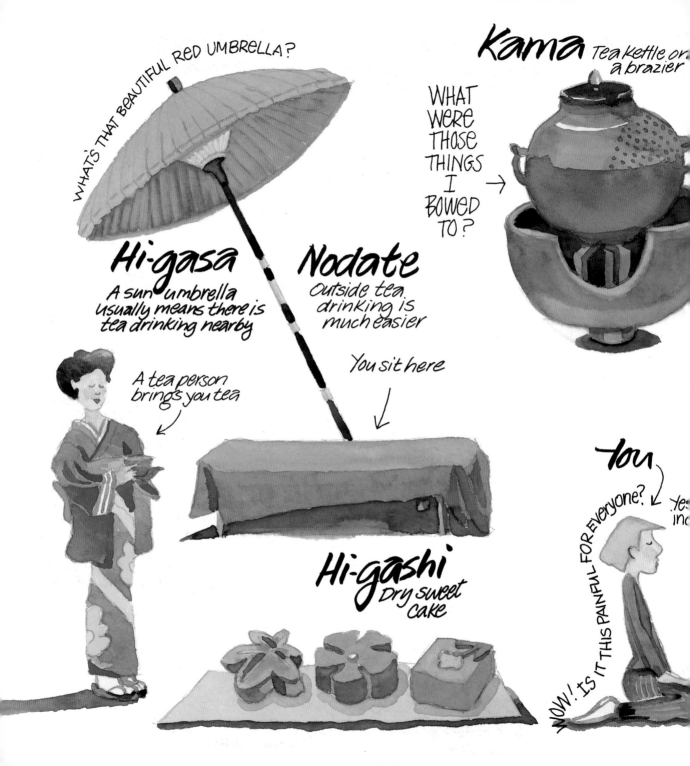

WHAT'S THAT BEAUTIFUL RED UMBRELLA?

Kama
Tea kettle or a brazier

WHAT WERE THOSE THINGS I BOWED TO? →

Hi-gasa
A sun umbrella usually means there is tea drinking nearby

Nodate
Outside tea drinking is much easier

A tea person brings you tea

You sit here

Hi-gashi
Dry sweet cake

You

WOW! IS IT THIS PAINFUL FOR EVERYONE?

Yes ind

Chasen
Tea whisk

Cha-ire
A tea container so expensive it comes with its own silk coat

Chasaku
Tea scoop

Cha-bana
Wild-flower arrangement

Sublime Tea Time
Chanoyu

At a traditional tea ceremony you sit motionless for hours while you admire everything and bow often. It's better to go with someone who knows what to do.

How to drink tea:
① Admire bowl. ② Turn bowl clockwise 180° so that the sacred spot faces away from you ③ Slurp your tea to show you like it. ④ Clean the rim with a cloth. ⑤ Turn bowl back counterclockwise 180°. ⑥ Admire the bowl again.

Try to NOT wear socks with holes

WHAT WAS ALL THAT TEA BOWL SWIRLING ABOUT?

Chawan
Tea bowl

DON'T THESE MEN EVER WEAR PANTS? When you're this big you can wear whatever you wa[...]

Higasa
Sun parasol
↓

Topknot

Yukata
Light cotton kimono
↓

Sagari
Stiffened silk co[...]

WHAT ARE THOSE PORCUPINE QUILLS AROUND HIS WAIST?

Geta
Wooden Clogs
↗

Bandages everywhere

Stunning Sumo Style

Keshō-mawashi
ceremonial apron donated by fans

Tsuna
Yes, the grand champion's ceremonial rope is four meters long, weighs fifteen kilos and is symbolic as well as decorative

WHAT IS THAT DO...

ISN'T THAT THE SAME ROPE I SEE AT SHRINES AND AROUND CEDAR TREES?

Bare feet

More Sumo Style

Mawashi
This silk belt is nine meters long, weighs five kilos and costs $3000

Oichō-mage
A hairstyle in the shape of a gingko leaf held in place by a fragrant pomade

The flipside of sumo is a real fashion risk

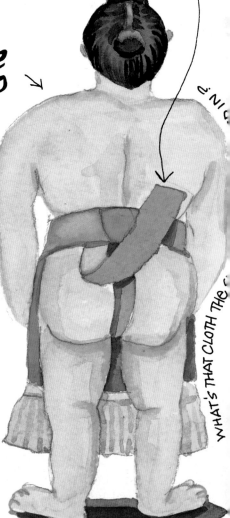

WHAT'S THAT CLOTH THE ...

Gyōji
Sumo referee (not to be confused with a gyōza, a pork dumpling)

Gunbai
War paddle

Yobidashi
He announces the contestants

Eboshi
Referee's hat

Dagger – (Just in case he makes a bad call)

HOWLING BETWEEN MATCHES?

WHO'S THAT FELLOW

Tattsuke-bakama
His working clothes

Jika-tabi
Split-toed shoes

The conformity look

The sleek look

The wide look

Schoolday dress is uniform from head to toe, but after class — anything goes!

$200 schoolbag

← Designer bag

←Telephone

Bustles

Platform boots

Lacy socks →

Kakko-ii
Chic Clothing

The minimal look ↓

The straight and narrow look ↓

The traditional look

The hip-hop look

↙ Chapatsu (dyed hair)

Fur piece

Kimono

Minuscule purses →

Micro-miniskirts

Zori

Platform sneakers ↓

Futon
At night maids lay out bedding for you to sleep on

Nihonma
Japanese room with tatami mat floors

Haori
Wool jacket

Yukata
A cotton kimono for after the bath

Remember to fold your Yukata left over right.

Leave your shoes at the entrance to the inn. Wear a pair of slippers to your room, but remove them before stepping on the tatami

Put on the toilet slippers when you enter the toilet

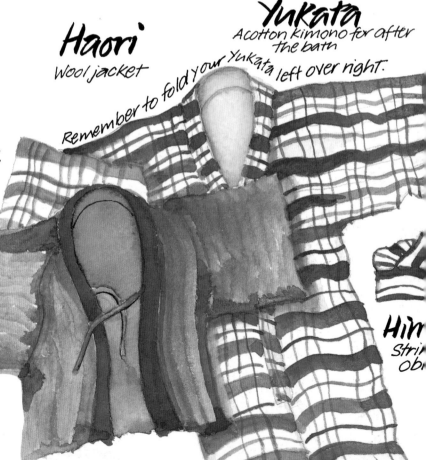

Toire-no-surippā
Toilet slippers

Hin
Stri
ob

An outside bath is called a rotenburo

You can wear your towel on your head

Tenugui

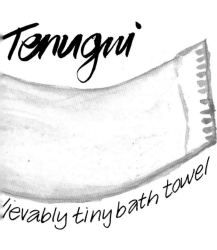

...ievably tiny bath towel

Ryokan
Japanese Inns

Furo
How to bathe:

① Please choose the correct room

女 男
Ladies   Gents

④ Fill the bucket with water and scrub yourself clean

⑤ Hose yourself clean before entering the bathtub

③ Sit on this

② Put your clothes in a basket

← The Total Look

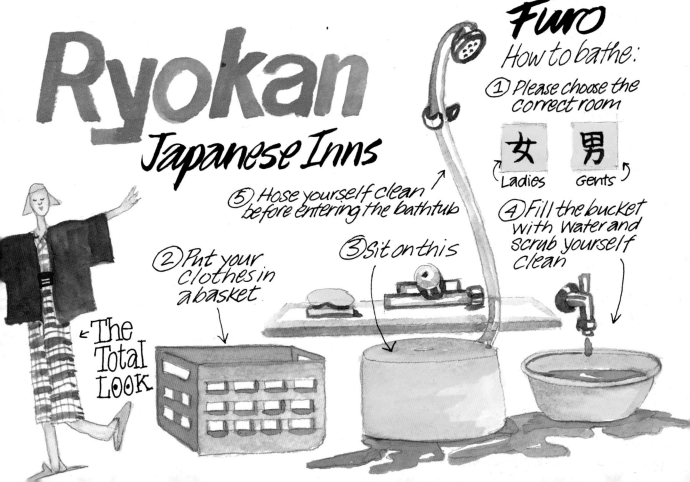

Ryokan Ryōri
Inn Cuisine

Ryokan meals are healthy, substantial and delicious. Bon Appetit!

Nabe
Hotpot with seafood and veggies

Takenoko
Bamboo shoots

Nama Tamago
Raw egg

Nattō
Sticky fermented beans

Och
Gre te

Gohan
Rice

Sarada
Salad

Miso-shiru
Soybean soup

Mochi
Fried rice cakes

N
D se

Tsuke
Pickle veggie

Yakizakana
Grilled fish

Atsuyaki Tamago
Sweet omelet

Hashi

chopsticks should always point to the left

Asagohan
Breakfast

Aisu Ti
Iced tea

Kōra
Cola

Miruku
Milk

Orenji Jūsu
Orange Juice

Ocha
Greentea

Kōcha
English tea

Kōhi
Coffee

Atsukan
Hot sake

Sake
Cold sake

M
W sa

Bangohan
Dinner

Ocha
Green tea →

Kudamono
Fruit

Nabe
Hotpot with meat and veggies

Tempura
Fried seafood and veggies ↓

Kani
Crab

Gohan
Rice

Shōyu
Soy sauce →

Wasabi Green horseradish

Sashimi
Raw fish ↑

**...me-
...shi**
...led
...s

Suimono
Clear soup →

**...sai-no-
...imono**
...iled veggies

Chawan-mushi
Steamed egg custard with a suprise inside

**...na
...iru**
...t beer

Biiru
Beer

Shōchū
Japanese vodka

Ringo Jūsu
Apple juice ↓

Mizu
water

Nomimono
Things to drink
You'll have to pay exta for everything but ocha and mizu

Rent-a-protest truck
You too can get behind a microphone and blast your views around Tokyo

white doilies on seats

White gloves

Takushii
A taxi
Never touch that door-it opens and closes automatic

Whole squads of gas station attendants hoot & hollar to welcome you

Your basic size non-Japanese person

Ban
Van

止まれ

日曜・祝日を除く
高・中速車
踏切注意
横風注意
動物注意
注意

前方優先道路

歩行者専用路
路肩弱し
騒音防止区間
歩行者横断あり
対向車多し
通学路

Can you read these traffic signs? Neither can I

Kuruma
Car
The small ones have names like mini, Guppie and Cappuccino

side of the road

ITENSHA
Cyclists ride on the pavement

IS THAT A CIRCUS TRUCK?

Reikyūsha
No, it's a very ornate hearse

Norimono-zukushi
Various Vehicles

NO STANDING OR STOPPING

Gomi-shūshūsha
Garbage trucks so tiny they can drive on the pavement

Mijetto tsū
The Midget II pick-up truck

THIS CONGESTED CITY

WHAT'S THAT MYSTERIOUS BUILDING SHAPED LIKE A LIPSTICK?

WHAT'S THAT BUILDING WITH AN ERECTION?

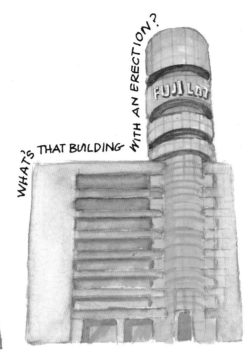

Tokyo Tower

Actually a radio tower built to top the Eiffel Tower

NOA Building

Houses the Fiji Embassy, a furniture store, a nightclub and various offices

Fuji Latex

The home of a condom manufacturer

WHAT'S THAT BUILDING WITH THE GIANT GOLDEN POO?

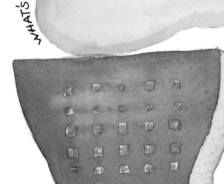

Super Dry Hall

The object on top is said to represent a frothy head and the burning heart of Asahi Beer

WHAT'S THE EIFFEL TOWER DOING IN TOKYO?

Megur Clu

A hotel that ren rooms b the hou

LOOKS LIKE A PENCIL SHARPENER?

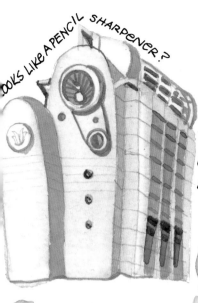

Wacoal Kojimachi Building
Home of Wacoal Lingerie

WHAT'S THAT WEIRD THING I SEE ON THE WAY TO THE AIRPORT?

LaLa Port Ski Dome
Tokyo's indoor ski slope

Kawatta Kenchiku
Amazing Architecture

PEEKING OVER THE ROOFTOPS?

Joule-A Building
Houses a sports-club, a school and various restaurants and offices

WHAT'S THAT BUILDING THAT LOOKS LIKE IT'S BURSTING APART AT THE SEAMS?

IS THAT THE WORLD'S LARGEST CAN OPENER?

Meguro Gajoen
A hotel, museum and office complex

Soft drinks—
they taste better
than they sound

Blue panels mean
cold drinks
Red panels mean
hot drinks

These machines
sell a variety
of merchandise:
support pantyhose,
$100 designer ties
and even live
flower arrangements

Having a party?
Take home a
half-gallon jug
of beer and a
three-pound
sack of rice!

Some
machin
have th
own nor
(entran
curtain

Sake
hot or
Cold

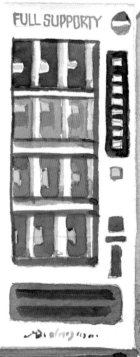

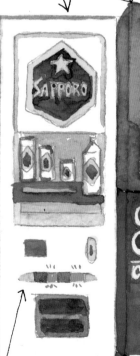

You can win a free drink
in a vending lottery

Jidōhanbaiki
Venerable Vending Machines

You never know when you'll need a battery →

Pornography is hidden behind a metallic curtain during the day and exposed at night →

24-hour condom service, categorized by blood type, believed an indicator of compatibility →

Schoolgirls' used panties (don't ask!) →

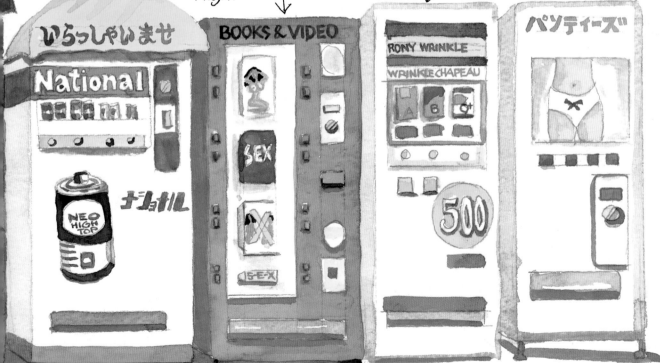

Toire
Terrifying Toilets

How to use an Eastern toilet:

① Find the right room

お手洗い	女子	男子
Toilet	Women's	Men's

② It's wise to bring your own tissues

③ If you see toilet slippers, put them on

④ Face the appliance and straddle it, then squat low. Go slowly to avoid splashing shoes

⑤ Activate the flush lever, which could be anywhere

⑥ Don't forget to remove the toilet slippers when you leave

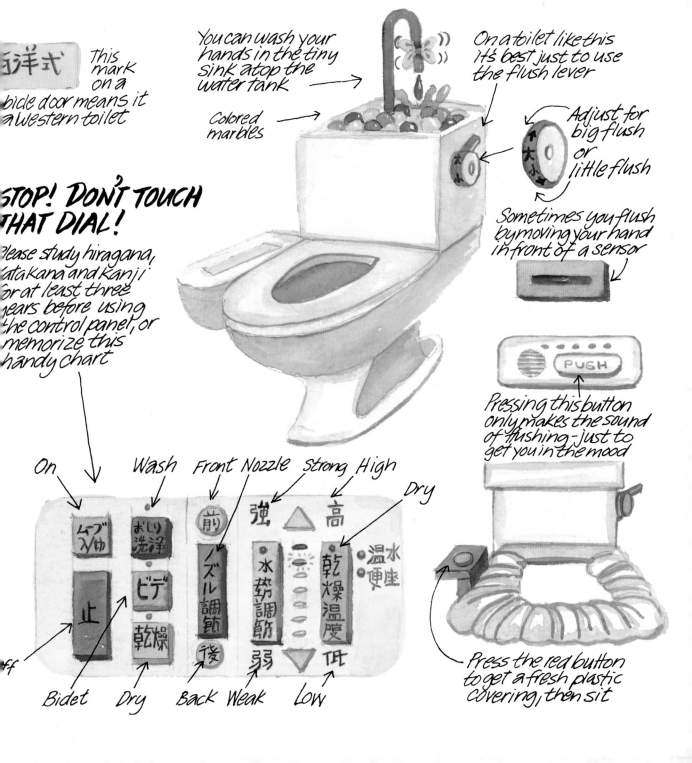

This mark on a bicle door means it a Western toilet

You can wash your hands in the tiny sink atop the water tank

Colored marbles

On a toilet like this it's best just to use the flush lever

Adjust for big flush or little flush

Sometimes you flush by moving your hand in front of a sensor

STOP! DON'T TOUCH THAT DIAL!

Please study hiragana, katakana and kanji for at least three years before using the control panel, or memorize this handy chart

Pressing this button only makes the sound of flushing - just to get you in the mood

PUSH

On
Wash
Front Nozzle Strong High
Dry

強 高

Off
止 ビデ 乾燥
前
水勢調節
乾燥温度
水座温便

後
弱 低

Bidet Dry Back Weak Low

Press the red button to get a fresh plastic covering, then sit

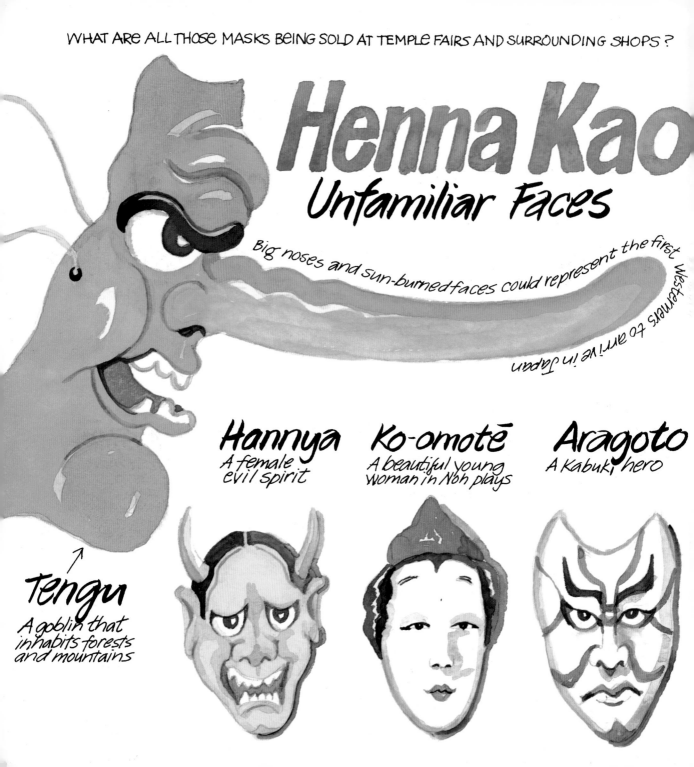

Henna Kao
Unfamiliar Faces

Big noses and sun-burned faces could represent the first westerners to arrive in Japan

Hannya
A female evil spirit

Ko-omoté
A beautiful young woman in Noh plays

Aragoto
A Kabuki hero

Tengu
A goblin that inhabits forests and mountains

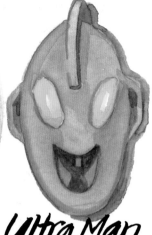

ailor Moon

ng, a teenage cartoon
ine fights for justice
an unfair world

An Pan Man

A Japanese Superboy,
named after a sweet
bean cake loses power
if his face gets dirty

Doraemon

A magical cat who
invents extraordinary
things

Ultra Man

An action figure
and Cartoon
hero

Inari Kitsune

Guardian of
the rice goddess

Hyotto-ko

This old man trying
to kindle a fire is often
paired with Okame

Okame

The goddess
of mirth

Kojō

An old man

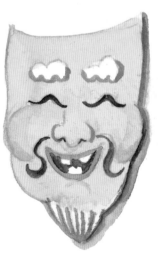

IS THAT STATUE BREATHING?

Put money here ↓

WHY WOULD ANYONE SPEND $50 to $100 ON LEFTOVER GOODS SIGHT UNSEEN?

福

5000円
10000円

I'm still clueless on this

Fuku Bukuro
"Happiness bags"

↑
Takuhatsu
An itinerant priest collecting alms

WHY DO MY NEIGHBORS LEAVE

Demae
They'll be picked up by the restaurant th delivered the meal

Two-Cup Ozeki
A bra that holds two generous servings of body warmed sake

Fushigi
Oddities and Entities

THOSE NICE MEN WITH THE WHITE GLOVES?

Shiri-oshi

"Tushy pushers" pack people into rush-hour trains

DISHES OUTSIDE THEIR FRONT DOOR?

IS THAT A HUMAN SIGN?

ストリップショウ

Hot bowls of food are held tight between these clamps

Demaeki
Delivery scooter

Sando-ichi man

"Sandwich men" frequently advertise sex shows

WHY DOES THE ELEVATOR OPERATOR SOUND LIKE MINNIE MOUSE?

Erebētā Gāru

Elevator girls affect childlike, high-pitched voices to sound more feminine and polite

THE GOOD WITCHES OF HARAJUKU DYE THEIR HAIR HOT PINK

ELVIS WANNABEES HAVE DANCED EVERY SUNDAY FOR THIRTY FORTY T...

Taped, worn-out boots

Harajuku Youth

Uranai-shi

Fortune tellers do a brisk business on the street, usually advising on matters of the heart

人相

WHY DO PEOPLE WEAR MASKS?

Masuku

Masks are worn prevent the s... of ger...

THEY KNOW WHEN THEY'VE ARRIVED AT THEIR STATION?

They don't—they often sleep right through it

Motto Fushigi
More Oddities and Entities

Chindonya
A noisy form of advertising for store openings and other events

Biru Bochi
Rooftop cemeteries are appearing due to shortage of space

WHAT ARE THOSE BIZARRE MINI PARADES?

Sayonara
Goodbye, until we see you in Tokyo

In truth, you cannot long remain totally clueless in Tokyo, for the more dazed and confused you appear, the sooner some kind person will come to your aid.

The "Weathermark" identifies this book as a production of Weatherhill, Inc., publishers of fine books on Asia and the Pacific. Original art and hand-lettered text by Betty Reynolds. Editorial supervision by Ray Furse. Production supervision by Bill Rose. Printed and bound in China by Oceanic Graphic Printing, Inc.

Shinkansen
A bullet train that goes so fast it makes your ears ring